A World in Change

# ELIZABETH AND AKBAR

**Portraits of Power**

## Annabel Wigner

Plumstead Manor School, London

Series editor: Rosemary Kelly

Resource Centre

This book aims to introduce you to a very old relationship: the relationship between Britain and India which began in the period that is called the Early Modern Age.

The links between these two countries are still important today, and affect the lives of us all. By studying the more familiar figure of Elizabeth I of England and comparing this with the lesser-known Akbar of India, we learn about a culture other than our own and develop an understanding of how other people live and what they value. We also get some idea of how a particular society has developed and in what ways it has changed or remained the same over centuries.

Elizabeth and Akbar were leaders of their countries during the sixteenth century, and there were many similarities in their lifestyles. They both had a great deal of power, and how they used their power is important. Sometimes they made good and just decisions; at other times they acted in a very cruel way. Both were born to rule, and by studying their lives we learn something of how rich and powerful people lived in the sixteenth century.

Stanley Thornes (Publishers) Ltd

# How to use this book

Different kinds of evidence have been used to produce a picture of the lives of Elizabeth and Akbar. These include extracts from diaries and travellers' tales, as well as the pictorial evidence of portraits, maps and objects in museums. Where possible, all the evidence included comes from people alive at the time. To make the meaning clearer, the spelling of many of the quotations has been modernised, but the wording is unchanged. We must remember, though, that people's beliefs may make them very one-sided witnesses. Apart from this, they may not actually have seen the events they describe; or if they did, they may not have seen *everything* that happened. If they seem to have relied on gossip, we must decide how much truth there is in that. In other words, we need to think about possible *bias* in the evidence, and how *accurate* it is.

It is important, too, to get clear in our minds the *order* in which important historical events happened, during the period covered by this book. We call this *chronology*.

This is a short book, and there is not enough space to include stories of the lives of the ordinary men and women that they ruled. We must remember that Elizabeth was not typical of women in the sixteenth century; the majority of women were not nearly as fortunate. There is still much that remains to be written about women in history to give us a clearer picture of women's lives in the past. Likewise Akbar was not a typical ruler. Few monarchs of this period have ever shown themselves to be as wise and understanding. It is important to realise that much has been omitted here because of lack of space. There are many facts to be discovered; there are still many areas of Indian history which have not been studied in full in this country. This book provides a beginning and there is a list of books at the end of each chapter from which further ideas can be developed.

---

*The picture on the front cover shows Akbar with a wild elephant, which has its back legs tied to a tree. Elephants were dangerous and had to be approached with caution.*

# A female ruler in an age of men

On 24 March 1603 a long procession began to wind its way through the streets of London. Over a thousand people dressed in hoods and suits of black followed a hearse on its way to Westminster Abbey. The coffin contained the body of Elizabeth I who had been Queen of England since 1558. Many people lined the streets, some of them in tears as they watched this last *progress*, or procession, pass by. One little girl, Lady Ann Clifford, was too small to join the procession. She recorded in her diary:

> When the corpse of Queen Elizabeth had continued at Whitehall as long as the Council had thought fit, it was carried to Westminster, the Lords and Ladies going on foot to attend it, my mother and my Aunt of Warwick being mourners, but I was not allowed to be one because I was not high enough, which did much trouble me then; but yet I stood in the church at Westminster to see the solemnity performed.

*In this picture you can see the litter (a type of stretcher) which carried the wax model of the dead Queen. She was shown dressed in royal robes and wearing the crown. The writing beside the flags reads:*

*'The chariott drawne by foure horses upon which charret stood the coffin covered with purple velvett and upon that the representation [the wax model], the Canopy borne by six knights.'*

Elizabeth had reigned as Queen for nearly fifty years. The fears of some people in England, who had thought that a woman as Queen would not be able to do her job as well as a man, had turned out to be groundless. Within a few years of James coming to the throne, Elizabeth had become part of a legend of English greatness. To understand at least some of Elizabeth's success as Queen, we need to bear in mind that she was a female ruler, at a time when most positions of power were given to men, and think about what this meant to Elizabeth, her court and her people.

When Elizabeth was born in 1533 her father, Henry VIII, stayed only long enough to hear that a girl had been born, and not a boy which he desperately wanted. By the time she was three, Henry's determination to have a son and heir led him to order the execution of Elizabeth's mother, Anne Boleyn, and to declare Elizabeth illegitimate (i.e. that he had not been legally married to Anne, and that Elizabeth could not, therefore, lay claim to the throne) so that he could marry Jane Seymour. After this, life for the young princess became a succession of new 'mothers'. During much of her childhood those who supervised her were kept short of money, and the young princess often went without new clothes and lacked proper care because she was out of favour at court. To survive the misery and danger of her childhood and adolescence was an achievement, and at the age of 25, with the charge of illegitimacy reversed, Elizabeth became the last child of Henry VIII to succeed to the English throne.

Elizabeth was not gentle in manner, nor was she quiet or shy. She was lively, outgoing and clever. The Spanish ambassador wrote that Elizabeth was 'more feared' than her stepsister, Mary, had been, and that she 'gave her orders and had her way absolutely as her father did'. Elizabeth's personality caused many of her advisers a problem. Even Robert Cecil, the Queen's Secretary and close friend, showed that he did not understand the Queen, when he scolded one of his department for discussing foreign policy with her — Cecil considered this to be 'too much for women's knowledge'. Most people considered that women were unfit to do anything except 'be made to keep home and to nourish their families and children, and not to meddle with matters abroad, nor to bear office in a city'.

If people found the new Queen's attitude difficult to understand, it is important to think about the problems the Queen herself faced as a female ruler, and how she was forced to behave. Daughters born to wealthy families in sixteenth-century society were under the control of their fathers until they married. If their husbands died, then control of their lives often passed back again to their fathers. We are used to thinking that money can give us a choice in the way we live our lives. But in the sixteenth century, a gift of houses, land, money and goods passed from the wife's family to the husband's in marriage settlements. This was called a *dowry*. If large amounts of money were involved in the marriage, fathers became even more careful in the choice of husband for their daughters, to make sure that the dowry passed into reliable hands.

*A miniature of Elizabeth I, painted shortly after she had inherited the throne of England*

*The artist, Levina Teerlinc, was a member of the group of women who were Gentlewomen of the Bedchamber. It is thought that she gave some training to a very famous miniaturist, Nicholas Hilliard.*

From the beginning, fathers took a keen interest in how their daughters were brought up, and Elizabeth was no exception. She was trained in all the activities which were considered suitable for young women. She was an excellent needlewoman, she could manage a large household, play several musical instruments and write well-composed letters. She was taught religious studies and good manners from an early age. Children were not allowed to talk at mealtimes unless spoken to and were expected to join in only on serious topics. Anything enjoyable which could be considered time-wasting was forbidden. From an early age, children had to behave as though they were adults, and were often beaten if they made the slightest mistake.

Because of her position in society Elizabeth's upbringing was particularly strict. Her education was wider than that of most other girls, because of the life she would lead as a member of the royal household. In Elizabeth's case her tutors were told that they were to watch her behaviour carefully. She was the daughter of Anne Boleyn who had been tried and executed because Henry had thought she had been unfaithful as a wife. Her family hoped that if she were very strictly disciplined that she would learn from this, and despise her mother. Elizabeth had a flair for languages, which were an essential part of education for a royal princess, and she was a gifted student. She studied with other young women of a similar social background, and pleased her tutors with her willingness and ability to learn.

Roger Ascham, one of Elizabeth's teachers, had this to say about her:

> French and Italian she speaks like English; Latin with fluency, care and judgment; she also spoke Greek with me . . .
>
> It is your shame (young gentlemen of England), that one girl should go beyond you all, in excellency of learning and knowledge of many languages. And that which is most praiseworthy of all she can understand, speak and write, both wittily with head and fair with hand.

Being teacher to a princess was a particularly good job, which Ascham would not want to lose, and he would be careful to praise Elizabeth's ability in his reports. Even so, there were many other people who wrote about Elizabeth and they all agreed that she was a talented woman.

**1** Why is it important to remember that Roger Ascham might write a biased report on Elizabeth?

**2** In what way is your education different from that of the young Elizabeth?

**3** Try writing your own school report. Make a list of the subjects that you study. Work out some general comments about your ability and achievement. Is your assessment of yourself different in any way from that of your teachers?

# The role of a rich Elizabethan woman

Elizabethan women were expected to marry, and to support their husbands by running a smooth and efficient household. It was also thought necessary for each family to have children; and the number of children should depend on how many the household could afford to support.

Look at the picture of William Brooke, 10th Lord Cobham, with his family. You will find a colour reproduction in the centre-section of the book. Lord Cobham's wife, Frances Brooke, is on the left of the picture. Her elder sister, Jane, is on the right.

What can we learn about rich Elizabethan families from looking at the picture of Lord Cobham and his family?

Here are some ideas to think about:

**1** How can you tell that this family is wealthy?

**2** Which child is shown as being the most important child in the family? (Look at the little boy on the left hand side of the picture, and see who is giving him some grapes.)

**3** In what ways does this picture show you how parents expected their children to behave when they were at the dinner table with adults?

**4** Which person in the picture controls this family?

**5** This picture shows a clear idea of the way an upper-class family was run in Elizabethan times. Try and find out the ways in which life would be different for boys and girls. In particular, you should look for information on education, pastimes, hobbies, job prospects and life at home.

**6** Now think about Elizabeth, as a young princess being taught to be a monarch. Do you think she would have found it hard to learn to behave like her father? Would you have enjoyed this type of education and life?

This sort of picture is very useful to us because it gives us so many things to think about. Obviously this is a wealthy family. Hiring an artist to paint a picture was far too expensive for poor people. Many people thought it was worth spending the money on a portrait like this to be able to show off to their friends and relations. All the family in the picture have dressed up for this special occasion. The parents have many children because this would have been expected in a family as wealthy as this. Since young girls in rich families would be brought up to expect many children of their own, it could cause much unhappiness if for any reason a woman did not have children or failed to produce a large family. (You could find out what happened to both Catherine of Aragon and Elizabeth's mother, Anne Boleyn.)

Today we use a special term for describing this kind of family. We call it a 'nuclear family', and it contains a mother, a father and the children. We can also show a nuclear family by using symbols instead of pictures, but it is better to use both. In the diagram below, the children have been put on the long line in order of age. You should read this from left to right.

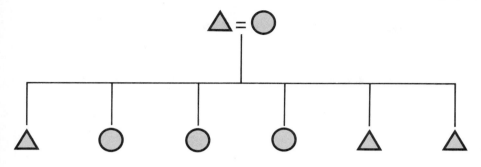

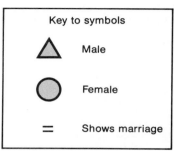

A diagram of the Cobham family

Now use the picture and the chart together.

**1** Look at the picture carefully and find the twins in the family.

**2** The eldest boy is six years old. His symbol is the first one on the left of the diagram. Where do the twins fit on the diagram?

**3** Decide which of the two small boys is the youngest, and find his place on the diagram.

**4** Now match the two remaining children on the diagram with the correct symbol, and you have found all the children on the chart.

The ages of the children are marked on the picture, but they are difficult to see unless you have a large and clear print. The original is at Longleat House. There may have been another child in the family, but the picture has been cut off on one side, and any evidence of a seventh child is missing.

After looking at evidence, either written extracts or pictures, it is always useful to think about what you have learned. In this way you will begin to understand the period you are studying more clearly.

# Wealth, power and status in the sixteenth century

It was usually the eldest male who inherited a title and most of the family property. See how this worked with Henry VIII's children (page 8), and look for the special symbols, which have been put in by the children's names. Write down the dates of their accession to the throne in chronological order.

For Mary and Elizabeth the major problem in their childhood was the fact that neither of them was a boy. Henry turned the running of the country upside down in order to get a male child.

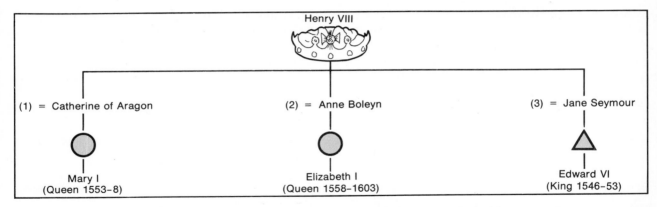

Henry VIII

(1) = Catherine of Aragon

Mary I
(Queen 1553–8)

(2) = Anne Boleyn

Elizabeth I
(Queen 1558–1603)

(3) = Jane Seymour

Edward VI
(King 1546–53)

Although titles and land passed first to the eldest son, in some cases women *were* able to inherit directly, and this happened with Mary and Elizabeth. But often even wealthy and important women found it difficult to have some choice in the way they led their lives in marriage, and were not free even when their husbands died. Living by themselves was something few women would have thought possible. When this did happen, having a lot of money helped a great deal.

Elizabeth chose not to marry and share her throne with a husband. She had seen that marriage had not worked for her father's wives or for her sister. By not marrying and not having children she broke the rules of the society which she governed. As Queen she had great power and a special status in England which, together with her forceful personality and Tudor inheritance, enabled her to make up her own rules. Other women with less power and status were not so fortunate. As children, they obeyed their fathers, and when they became wives they obeyed their husbands.

Elizabeth I inherited much more power as Queen of England than our present monarch. The picture on the left will help you understand how important a monarch was in the sixteenth century.

*The picture shows Elizabeth juggling with clubs which represent her subjects*

You will see from the picture that the largest club represents the people that Elizabethans called the *Fourth Sort*. These were the ordinary people of the country, labourers for example. There were more people in this group than in all the others added together. The *Second* and *Third Sorts* were composed of merchants, businessmen, craftsmen, scholars, lawyers and ordinary gentry. The richest and most powerful people (the *First Sort*) were very small in number and formed the government of the country and held all the important positions in the church or at court. Elizabeth had real power and used it unhesitatingly. This kind of power was based on the idea that God had set out a special sort of order, which gave all ruling families power over everyone else.

Since all wealth and power came from the Queen, it was to the Court of Elizabeth that people travelled if they hoped to improve their position in society.

People did not always stay in the 'sort' into which they had been born. The following diagram shows the ladder of success in Elizabethan England and how a person could rise, or fall, from one 'sort' to another.

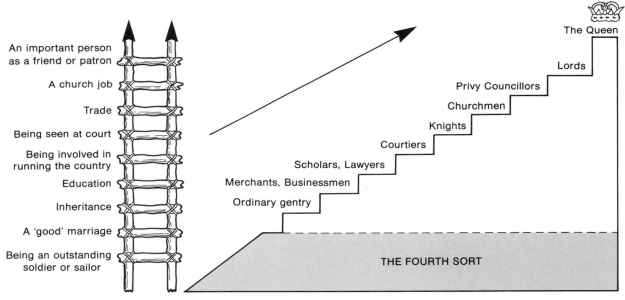

*Some ways of climbing the Elizabethan ladder of success*

For further reading:
D Mountfield, *Everyday Life in Elizabethan England* (Liber, 1978)
J Fines, *Tudor People* (Batsford, 1977)
R Kelly, *A World of Change* (Stanley Thornes, 1987)
T Kelly, *Children in Tudor England* (Stanley Thornes, 1987)

Visit:
The Museum of London, London Wall

# Understanding your family tree

You have your own history, which is special to you and your family. No one family is like any other. One of the most enjoyable ways of getting to understand how you fit into the world in which you live is to keep a record of all the interesting things your family has experienced. This is how you could begin.

Design your own family tree. Try to get photographs of *your* 'nuclear family' and draw your own diagram. Take your 'tree' back as far as your great-grand-parents, and arrange the names and dates of births (and deaths) in a clear, correct order. Make certain that all your facts are accurate. Add your photographs, and family symbols for male and female.

## Doing oral history

Draw up a list of questions to ask your parents and grandparents. Interviewing people looks easy on television but is actually very difficult. You need to prepare carefully if you want to get the right sort of information. If you have not got a tape recorder, you will have to use a notebook and pencil.

All the way through this book you will see quotations and pictures being used as evidence to show what life was like for Elizabeth and Akbar. The information you collect from your family's memories can be used in the same way. Begin collecting your facts from your family; and then ask them to tell you their thoughts on their childhood and adolescence, their schooling and their first job. Make a note of things they have not told you, and ask them about those also. Write your notes into your own history, and then go on to things about how your family fits into the area in which you live. For example, has your family always lived in the same area? If not, where did they come from?

Imagine that you are living in the year 2086. In the attic of the house where you live, you find a chest full of things that your family put on one side in the twentieth century.

1. What does your chest contain? (Here are a few ideas for things you could have in your chest: a broken Walkman, a pack of cards, a photograph album, a pair of shoes, a diary, two children's books, a set of beads, postcards of Spain, a chipped vase.)

2. How would you find out about how these things were used?

3. How would you date them?

4. Why were these things stored in the attic at all?

5. Which of these things would you pick to form part of a museum display? What other items would you include in your display if you wanted to give people a clear idea about the way families lived in the twentieth century?

# Life at the top

The centre of the world of the Elizabethan court was London. If we were visiting the London of the sixteenth century, and travelling up the river Thames from the coast, the skyline that would greet us would seem very different from today. Most of the important buildings were squashed up together on the northern bank of the river. The only built-up area on the southern side contained the site of the Globe Theatre, a few houses and Southwark church. The most impressive feature might seem to be London Bridge. This part of Elizabethan London was admired for its architectural design, but renowned perhaps most of all for its solemn warning to Londoners of the power of the Crown: any subjects falling out of favour with the Queen were quite likely to be executed and their heads placed on spikes at the southern end of London Bridge.

*The heads of some of Elizabeth's more unfortunate subjects on display on London Bridge*

*It must have been very frightening and gruesome to see, with all the birds of prey hovering over the rotting flesh.*

The Thames was a busy waterway. London streets and roads in and out of the city were extremely bad. The Queen used the river a great deal, as it was a very comfortable way of travelling. One of her favourite journeys was the river passage to Richmond Palace. Her barge had cushions made of cloth of gold, and there was a crimson velvet rug to keep her feet warm. Flowers would be put over the floor to sweeten the air, and she could look out of the glass windows of the cabin as she travelled.

Elizabeth had inherited many palaces, most of them within easy reach of London. In these, and in the splendid houses of her subjects, she held court. The mixture of business and pleasure was a standard part of the routine of the court day. Government work and administration of the country, feasts for important people, the celebration of special occasions, and the custom of service to the crown, centred on the presence of the Queen. When she moved from one royal residence to another, dispatch boxes were rushed up and down the country, following the Queen as she travelled. It was much harder to organise the running of the country when the Queen was moving around, and this caused her ministers a great deal of worry.

In the centre of London, surrounded by the homes of the nobles, was the Queen's Palace of Whitehall. It was regularly open to visitors, and people were able to tour round any part of the Queen's property. This sounds strange to us, as very few of us today would be allowed inside any royal buildings, and certainly not inside Buckingham Palace, without very special permission. People are much more security-conscious today. Although there were several assassination attempts against Elizabeth, she still allowed herself to take risks with her life, rather than seeming to be afraid to walk or ride among the people she ruled.

*In this picture of Whitehall Palace, drawn in 1555, you can see the river gateway.*

De Maisse was an ambassador in London in 1597. He was taken by river to Whitehall Palace and wrote this in his diary:

> The entrance on the riverside is very small and inconvenient; it is a covered alley and rather dark. It is very low and has no great appearance for a royal house.

De Maisse was obviously disappointed with this entrance, but approved of the main gate on the street side of the palace, which was much grander. When the Queen was not in residence at Whitehall, all her things travelled with her. If there was a visitor to Whitehall who was particularly important and needed to be impressed, then some of the special hangings would be sent back.

The Palace had three blocks which contained gardens, tennis courts, the Privy Chamber, the council chamber, a guard room and great hall, and the state apartments which contained Elizabeth's bedroom and bathroom. Elizabeth's bed was made of many different coloured woods, and had silk and velvet quilts decorated with gold and silver embroidery. All around the bed were curtains made of Indian silk which had been hand-painted.

She had a silver table on which she kept her jewellery box, and a chair made up of cushions piled up on the floor. It must have been a very dark room as there was only one small window; but she could look directly out onto the river from her apartments and enjoy the view, and could also spend time on the river when it was too hot to stay in her room.

Elizabeth always spent the months of July and August away from London when fears of the plague were widespread, and returned to take up residence at Whitehall again for the winter months. When she arrived, the streets of London were full of people waiting to greet her, and the Mayor and City Council arranged many exciting displays to welcome their Queen back to her capital city.

*The Queen on the way to her coronation*

*This is the kind of special procession that she liked to have organised for her.*

The Queen's personal guard, the Gentlemen Pensioners, marched with her, and so did the squires and footmen. You will see from the picture that no one is wearing a hat. In court and around the Queen no one was allowed to wear a hat, as it was considered respectful to be bare-headed in the presence of royalty.

# The knights of the Queen

Whitehall was not Elizabeth's favourite palace, but it was the centre for the celebrations held on three special days in England: Elizabeth's birthday, 7 September; her Accession Day, 17 November; and, after the defeat of the Spanish Armada in 1588, 19 November as well. These three days were celebrated all over the country, with church bells ringing, bonfires, fireworks and feasts. The main attraction in London, however, was the Whitehall Tilt, a spectacular tournament where two knights on horseback charged towards each other and attempted to break their opponent's tilting lance. Crowds of people flocked to the tiltyard to see this popular event. Even the ordinary Londoners were allowed in. They paid a shilling to watch the entertainment and, although this was very expensive, the stands were always full of people.

The events were organised by the Queen's Champion. The idea of knights in armour fighting in honour of their Queen sounds old-fashioned, and it was. Elizabeth liked such ideas, and in some ways behaved just like a medieval king. But she was also a Renaissance monarch, and the courts of European rulers in the sixteenth century were full of splendid displays. Courtiers gave Elizabeth expensive entertainment, beautiful presents, flattered her constantly, and fought for her favour at the tournaments. One of the Queen's greatest champions, the Earl of Cumberland, had the Queen's glove fixed on his hat and wore it all the time. It must have annoyed his wife enormously, but perhaps it was wiser not to make a fuss about something so important as his career.

Finding out about the Whitehall Tilt is quite difficult, because there is little evidence which survives from the Elizabethan period on this part of court life. You will have to use some detective skills to fit the pieces together properly.

The drawing on the next page shows George Clifford, Earl of Cumberland, as the Queen's Champion.

See if you can work out some of the things that this picture tells you about this particular Champion of the Whitehall Tilt:

**1** In his hand George Clifford is holding his tilting lance. How would he have used this?

*George Clifford, Champion of the Whitehall Tilt*

**2** His costume seems a little strange if he is going to fight in it. Can you think of another court occasion on which he could have worn this?

**3** What can you see fixed to his hat?

**4** His wooden shield which is hanging on a tree has a design on it. Can you see what it is?

**5** On the floor at his feet you can see his gauntlet (glove) and helmet. What did it mean when a knight threw down his gauntlet?

**6** As Champion of the Accession Day Tilt, for whose honour was he fighting?

**1** Look carefully at the Earl of Cumberland's armour. This armour is very decorative and would only be used on formal ceremonial occasions. What changes had occurred in methods of warfare over the fifteenth and sixteenth centuries to make armour such as this outdated in battle?

**2** On the armour there are gold lily flowers and roses. To which two countries do these flowers refer?

**3** In some books you will read that knights wearing their armour were so heavy that they had to be winched onto their horses. Do you think that this can be true?

**4** The armour would need to be made carefully in order for the knight to be able to move around. Look closely at the drawing and try and work out where the joints would have to be most flexible.

**5** Of what material would this suit of armour have been made?

**6** How would it have been fixed together?

*This drawing of the Earl of Cumberland's armour comes from a book of armour designs which is in the Victoria and Albert Museum. The suit of armour is in an American museum. The special shields carried by the knights would hang in the long gallery of Whitehall each year after the Tilt.*

Von Wedel, a German traveller, described the 1584 Tilt in his diary. Here is a translation of part of his account:

> The combatants had their servants clad in different colours. Some of the servants were disguised like savages ... others had horses equipped like elephants, some carriages were drawn by men, others appeared to move by themselves. The costs amounted to several thousand pounds each.

He was watching a kind of carnival procession with floats. All the people taking part had special costumes and were disguised. This would have cost a lot of money. If members of the court wanted to make a big impression they would have to spend a lot of money just for one appearance at the Tilt.

The Queen's favourite colours were black and white. Very often her knights arranged their display in those two colours and wore armour to match.

As each display made its way into the Tiltyard it would stop below the gallery to acknowledge the presence of the Queen. Funny speeches, music and poetry were written to amuse her before the tilting began, and then the knights would prepare themselves for combat. The score cheque was kept to show how many times the knights had run at each other, and how many lances had been shattered. The knight who broke his opponent's weapon completely scored the highest marks.

*This picture is thought to be of the Earl of Essex. As a courtier he pines for the love of Elizabeth and is dressed in her favourite colours to flatter her.*

*The Earl of Essex at the Accession Day Tilt of 1590*

## The Queen of the Whitehall Tilt

If you turn to the colour section at the centre of this book you will see the Ditchley Portrait of Elizabeth. This was painted in 1590 to mark Sir Henry Lee's retirement as Champion of the Tilt, and hung in his home at Ditchley near Oxford. It is now in the National Portrait Gallery. There are all sorts of symbols in it, some of which you will understand already; others will be new. Look at the picture and compare it with the descriptions below. All of the written evidence comes from De Maisse's diary. He admired the Queen, got on well with her, and kept a careful record of his meetings with her:

> On her head she wore a great reddish colour wig and hanging down over her forehead some pearls.

> As for her face, it is and appears to be very aged. It is long and thin, and her teeth are very yellow and unequal.

> Her figure is fair and tall and graceful in whatever she does. When anyone speaks of her beauty she says that she never was beautiful, although she had that reputation thirty years ago. Nevertheless she speaks of her beauty as often as she can.

**1** In this picture Elizabeth is shown as a powerful queen against the outline of the globe of the world. What events had happened to make Elizabethans feel particularly proud of their Queen?

**2** In many portraits of Elizabeth she is wearing a rose. In this one there is a pink rose pinned to her collar. What does this have to do with the Houses of York and Lancaster?

**3** Why do you think the sky is shown to be sunny on one side and dark on the other?

**4** There is something wrong with her waist and her feet. (Put a ruler from the middle of Elizabeth's face in a straight line to her feet.) What has the artist done incorrectly?

**5** When was Elizabeth born? Check again the date when this picture was painted. Does Elizabeth look her age?

**6** Compare the visual and written evidence of Elizabeth. From which do you feel you have learned the most?

**7** Pick your favourite piece of source material in this chapter. Write down all the reasons why it is your favourite, and write a paragraph to explain what you have learned from it.

Elizabeth made certain that the ordinary people she ruled felt that she took a special interest in them too. When she moved around London or went on progress through the countryside she spent time with them, and often stayed in the large country homes of her courtiers. Messages were sent out to warn of the Queen's possible arrival, and her servants would check that there would be enough accommodation and food supplies for everyone.

Most large houses could supply everything needed during the year for the household from goods produced on the estates, but the Queen's arrival meant that special quarters had to be put aside for her; the whole court had to be fed and provided with drink, and sleeping arrangements had to be made for everyone.

When the Queen travelled she used a litter or a coach. Sometimes she went on horseback for part of the journey. All the treasures had to be packed and countless personal items boxed up. In 1583 she ordered a new bed which was designed so that it could come apart and travel with her on her progresses. She generally arrived about six o'clock in the evening, in time for a meal, entertainment and a night's rest. She would expect only the best to be offered, and hospitality would include presents for her too. Sometimes, when the beer and food were poor and the presents were not good enough, Elizabeth would be ill-tempered and everyone would suffer as a result.

Sir Henry Lee, Champion of the Tilts, entertained the Queen in 1575 and 1592. He had won this special position at court by being an outstanding horseman. Lee arranged for the Queen to see a play, and then the Queen and her party were led to a specially-made banqueting house which had been built on a hill within the woods. Under a huge oak tree the Queen sat down to eat, and above her head hung ivy, flowers and decorations of gold. It must have made Elizabeth's memories of Oxfordshire much more happy. She had been kept as prisoner at Woodstock during Mary's reign and had lived in only three rooms. She used a diamond to scratch this poem on the window pane at Woodstock:

Much suspected, of me
nothing proved can be.
Quoth Elizabeth, Prisoner.

Sir Henry Lee's entertainment proved very successful. When the Queen visited him again at Ditchley 17 years later, Lee had retired as Champion. Tilting was very hard work, and he thought that at 47 he was too old to be Champion. At the 1590 Tilt, after his last fight, Lee took off his armour and put it on George Clifford. He then buttoned up a new black velvet coat and put on a country hat to show everyone that he was leaving court life. His days of fighting were over, but the Ditchley portrait reminded him of his days at the Whitehall Tilt.

For further reading:
P Glanville, *Tudor London* (Museum of London, 1979)
R Barber, *Tournaments* (Kestrel, 1978)
R Barber, *Arms and Armour* (Brockhampton Press)

Visit:
The Tower of London

# The Queen and her artists

*A miniature of Elizabeth I, painted in 1592*

*It was important to flatter your patron. This picture did not do that. Isaac Oliver, the artist, lost the Queen's patronage.*

*A seal for official documents*

*The face pattern could be used for a picture, a seal or a coin.*

Life at court in the reign of Elizabeth was based upon being in favour with the Queen, or with her favourite courtiers. All talented young people knew that they would get a good job in England if they were successful in finding someone powerful or rich enough to help them at court. A man or woman wealthy enough to provide such help was called a patron. A patron could provide an artist or writer with an allowance, materials with which to work, and workshop facilities.

Unlike other rulers in sixteenth-century Europe Elizabeth did not sponsor many young or talented people. This was because she could not afford to spend a lot of money on new palaces, works of art or the interior decoration of her favourite homes. But even though she rarely sponsored artists or builders herself, she could influence others who did, and it was important to pick a patron carefully. If an artist or writer selected a patron who lost favour with the Queen, everyone connected with that person suffered as well.

For artists painting portraits of the Queen there were very strict rules. In 1563 a royal proclamation was issued, which said that the Queen's picture could only be produced from a pattern of which the Queen approved. An artist of the Queen's choice, who produced a painting which the Queen liked, would then give the face pattern to other artists to use.

An artist would use one of these patterns for painting a picture, in a way very similar to the one we use to produce clothes today. Once a pattern had been made, hundreds of copies could be produced for portraits, miniatures and cameos for the wealthy, or medallions for the poor. The same 'face' could be used on state documents, seals and coins, and for book illustrations and pamphlets. Elizabeth knew it was important to impress everyone in England, and that is why she was so careful in her choice of a face pattern.

Studying portraits of Elizabeth I to find out whether they give a true picture of what she was like is really detective work, as we need to think of many things at once. Changes in fashion, dating of sources, style of ruffs, political affairs at home and abroad, and artists' impressions are just a few of the things we need to consider when we are looking at pictures of Elizabeth. It can be difficult to balance the information we see and read about Elizabeth as Queen. Many of the ideas we have of her reign have been handed down to us from people who looked back at her as a symbol of a wonderful and exciting age in English history; and this has given us a very biased viewpoint. We need to examine the bias we see both in pictures and in written sources, and try to find the real Elizabeth by balancing the evidence where it is conflicting. The evidence in this chapter has been selected to show you some of the problems historians have to deal with when detecting bias. As you read, see if you can match the written descriptions to the pictures and see how they differ.

# Elizabeth as the Moon Goddess

You will have seen many portraits of Elizabeth I but the Rainbow Portrait below may not be as familiar.

*A miniature of Elizabeth I (above), painted in 1586 or 1587*

*She is shown as Cynthia, Goddess of the Moon. The artist, Nicholas Hilliard, painted the Queen as eternally young, and she approved of his work.*

*The Rainbow Portrait, painted by Zucchero*

*Elizabeth is shown as Cynthia, Goddess of the Moon. In her headdress there is a small moon.*

Like the Ditchley Portrait which you will have seen in the centre-section of the book, the Rainbow Portrait was painted when Elizabeth was old. The double ruff can be dated to 1600, and so the picture was painted at that time. It is called the Rainbow Portrait because she is holding a rainbow in her hand. What do you think the artist is telling you about Elizabeth and the rainbow?

The huge ruff she is wearing caused problems at court. If every woman had worn one, it would have been quite dangerous! At one point they were banned from court dress. Look carefully at Elizabeth's head-dress. You will see that there is a crescent moon attached to it. This tells us that Elizabeth has been painted as the Goddess of the Moon. Many of the poems, plays and portraits of the Elizabethan age make reference to Greek myths and legends. The study of classical Greek was part of a child's education in the sixteenth century, and many people would have known the stories and legends from the past. Here are two verses from a poem written in honour of the Goddess of the Moon and of the Hunt:

Queen and huntress, chaste and fair,
Now the sun is laid to sleep,
Seated in thy silver chair,
*State* in *wonted* manner keep:
    *Hesperus* entreats thy light,
    Goddess excellently bright.

*the world, usual*
*the star Venus*

Earth, let not thy envious shade
Dare itself to *interpose*;
Cynthia's shining orb was made
Heaven to clear when day did close:
    Bless us then with wished sight,
    Goddess excellently bright.

*move across in front of the moon*

**1** Pinned to her ruff is a tiny gauntlet. To what special occasion in the Elizabethan year could this refer?

Elizabeth is wearing her favourite pearls, both in her hair and as bracelets and necklaces. Her dress is embroidered with spring flowers. Elizabethans had all sorts of decorations on their costumes. The following extracts come from the wardrobe list of Elizabeth's clothes:

A Petticoat.
Item, one petticoat of white satin, embroidered . . . with a very fair border of pomegranates, pineapple trees, and other fruits, and the nine *Muses*, in the same border.

*goddesses of the arts*

A Round Gown.
Item, one *round gown* of white cloth of silver, with works of yellow silk, like flies, worms and snails.

*full skirted dress*

A Cloak.
Item, one Dutch cloak of black velvet embroidered all over with flowers and grasshoppers.

20

**2** Make a list of things embroidered on Elizabeth's clothes.

**3** All over Elizabeth's cloak you can see eyes and ears. This tells us that Elizabeth could see and hear everything usually with the help of her advisers, and was very wise. The serpent on her sleeve symbolised her wisdom. In its mouth is a heart. What do you think this means?

**4** What other things does a serpent represent?

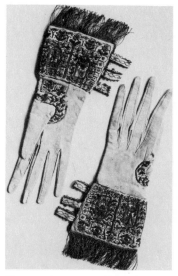

These gloves are thought to have belonged to Elizabeth I.

The cloak is of gold satin. Her other favourite colours were brown, yellow and different kinds of orange. She chose colours which went well with her auburn hair. Akbar's favourite colours were white, yellow and purple.

Elizabeth's make-up contained white of egg, powdered eggshell, borax, poppy seeds and alum. This had the effect of making her look younger than she was. All Elizabeth's artists painted her hands carefully. Elizabeth had beautiful hands and was fond of showing them off:

> She drew off her glove and showd me her hand, which is very long and more than mine by three broad fingers.
>
> *Seigneur de Maurier*

The following description was written in May 1557, just before Elizabeth inherited the throne:

> She is a young woman whose mind is considered no less excellent than her person, although her face is comely rather than handsome, but she is tall and well formed with a good skin although swarthy; she has fine eyes and above all a beautiful hand of which she makes a display.
>
> *Giovanni Michiel*

Here is an 'eye-witness' description of her when she was old:

> her face oblong, fair but wrinkled; her eyes small, yet black and pleasant, her nose a little hooked; her lips narrow, and her teeth black . . .; she wore false hair and that red
>
> *Paul Hentzner*

Read the descriptions carefully and look at the portrait.

**1** How old was Elizabeth when the Rainbow Portrait was painted?

**2** Compare the written evidence. How has Elizabeth changed in appearance?

**3** Why would Elizabeth and her councillors want everybody to think of Elizabeth as being younger than her actual age?

**4** Why would they like her to be painted as a Goddess?

**5** Draw your own 'Elizabeth I' face pattern in the sixteenth-century way, as has been shown in the picture of the Armada Portrait. Add jewels, decorate her ruff and put on her make-up.

*A twentieth-century copy of the Armada Portrait*

**6** How does the way Elizabeth used her clothes make her appear more important?

**7** The Rainbow Portrait shows Elizabeth dressed in a very strange costume. Here is a list of Elizabeth's favourite pastimes:

Walking, hunting, dancing, listening to music and playing instruments, acting in masques (a mixture of dancing, music and theatre), plays, embroidery, flowers and gardens, and gambling.

For which of these activities would this costume have been designed?

# Court life in miniature

As well as portraits of Elizabeth we have another set of pictures to show us the Queen and her court. On special occasions such as anniversaries, or at Christmas or the New Year, it became a custom to give miniature paintings, especially when it was known that the Queen liked them.

We appreciate the talent and creativity of artists today much more than many of the people of Elizabeth's court did. A court artist in the sixteenth century might have had to paint fences as well as faces in order to earn a living!

Sixteenth-century playing cards had a plain white side which was rubbed down. Fine parchment was then glued onto it. Brushes, made from squirrels' tails fitted into birds' quills and mounted into sticks, were used. Colours were mixed in mussel shells with gum arabic (a gum obtained from acacia plants), or sometimes sugar candy or ear wax. Animals' teeth were used for giving a polished appearance to the picture. Everything had to be kept very clean.

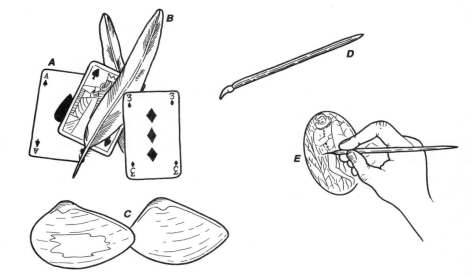

To make a miniature painting an Elizabethan miniaturist would work with all these tools:

**A** card – often a playing card
**B** quill – used for making brushes
**C** mussel shell – for mixing paint
**D** squirrel hair brush
**E** animal tooth set in handle, for burnishing

Try your own Elizabethan miniature; make sure your playing card is not too worn. Fix cartridge paper to it carefully so that you have a plain surface. Work in pairs and use each other as models! For research work on Elizabethan costume, look at the miniature paintings by Levina Teerlinc, Nicholas Hilliard and Isaac Oliver. Be sure to get the historical details of the dress as accurate as possible. You will find that painting in miniature is a very special art skill, so you might like to ask your art teacher for help. Both England and India have a tradition of miniature painting. Europeans took the idea of the use of perspective (an impression of depth and distance in a picture, in contrast to a rather 'flat' look) to Akbar's court, as well as some ideas for new subjects, and Indian artists were very interested. Look carefully at all the illustrations in this book, and compare the different styles of the visual evidence shown. Here are some things to think about: use of colour, use of symbols, subject matter, story telling, animals, birds and people, bias and historical accuracy, the use of perspective painting.

Large art reference books will give you good pictures to look at, but it is always better to see some originals if you can. There are pictures of Elizabeth in private collections, but many large galleries will have some for you to look at. You would enjoy a visit to the National Portrait Gallery in London. The Victoria and Albert Museum contains the largest collection of both English and Indian miniatures.

For further reading:
R Strong and J Oman, *Elizabeth R* (Secker and Warburg, 1971)
E Freeman, *Tudor Life and Dress* (Thomas Nelson, 1981)
*Queen Elizabeth I Paper Dolls to Colour* (Bellerophon Books, 1981)

Visits:
The National Portrait Gallery, London
The Victoria and Albert Museum, London

# European involvement with the East

When Thomas Platter was in London he visited the house of a man called Mr Cope, who was famous among the people of the area in which he lived, because he had been on a voyage to India. Platter was so interested in the many curious things he saw in Mr Cope's house that he made a list of them in his diary. Here are just a few of them:

> an African charm made of teeth; beautiful coats from Arabia; a fan made of a single leaf; a little box and porcelain from China; a Madonna made of Indian feathers; a mirror which both reflects and multiplies objects; two dyed Indian sheepskins with a silken sheen.

Tourism in the sixteenth century was not as easy as it is today. Travelling to the East involved a long and dangerous journey that might take as long as two years, if the route went overland. If all went well at sea, a ship could make the journey in nine months; but the hazards from treacherous currents, monsoons and storms, and attacks from pirates, meant that many ships were lost without trace. The desire to buy goods from the East and sell them in the markets of Europe was so great, that merchants and sailors were prepared to invest their money in trade, despite the risks involved.

English merchants joined the race to the East later than the other European countries of Portugal, Spain and the Netherlands. When Francis Drake sailed right round the world between 1577 and 1580 he proved that English ships and sailors were experienced enough at sea to be able to take part in the competition for markets in the East.

In the early sixteenth century the Portuguese had built up very strong trading links with India, China and Japan, and ruthlessly protected their right to trade by attacking any foreign ships they met. By the time of Elizabeth's reign religious changes in Europe had created divisions between many European countries, and there was fierce competition among them all to secure trade with the East. There was by now a Spanish stronghold in the Caribbean, and the Portuguese controlled the sea lanes leading to India via Africa and the overland route through the Persian Gulf. There were also Portuguese settlements in the East. English and Dutch privateers used their naval strength to attack the power of this Catholic control; they also attacked the Portuguese settlements in the East. Gold and silver from the

An Indian jeweller with his wares

*The portrait of Elizabeth I known as the Ditchley Portrait, painted by Marcus Gheeraerts the Younger (see pages 16 and 20)*

*William Brooke, 10th Lord Cobham, with his family, attributed to Hans Eworth (see pages 6 and 7)*

*A miniature showing the Queen performing the ancient custom of washing the feet of poor women, called the Maundy Ceremony, painted by Levina Teerlinc in 1565*

*A famous miniature, called the Heneage Jewel*

*The miniature has a richly decorated box and was painted by Nicholas Hilliard in 1600.*

*Akbar inspecting the building of his palace at Fatehpur Sikri (see pages 32–6)*

*Akbar helping lift a captured cheetah*

*Prince Salim and friends in a Mughal garden*

*Akbar's son, Jahangir, weighing Prince Khurram*

*Akbar in a hunting circle*

*All the illustrations on this page come from Indian miniatures which were book illustrations. They show some aspects of life at court in Mughal India.*

West, and shipments of spices, silk, perfumes, carpets and jewels from the East were rich prizes worth capturing.

The major goods which were exchanged around the trading area of the Middle East, India, China and Japan were silk, porcelain, sandalwood, black pepper, horses, ivory, silver, indigo, textiles and metal goods. In the large trading areas it was mainly the Portuguese merchants at this time who brought the goods back for the ever-growing European market. There was an English company already trading in the Eastern Mediterranean which was extremely profitable. It was therefore up to the businessmen and merchants living in the major trading centres of England to organise themselves into companies which could take them further afield than before.

Rich merchants were expanding the consumer market in London; many wealthy people were very willing to spend their money on these exciting new goods from foreign lands. New shops selling luxury goods did a flourishing trade, and the Royal Exchange, which was opened by Elizabeth, displayed a wide range of things which appealed to the tastes of the court and high society. Rich people were delighted with the number of fashionable things that they could buy.

In Cheapside, a famous silk merchant called Mr Hicks set up in business, with a white bear hanging outside to advertise his shop. He sold cloth of gold and silver, taffeta, satin and silk from Naples, velvets from Genoa, and silk from China. He grew very rich by selling his goods to those who lived at court.

In 1583 a ship set sail from England. On board was a London merchant called Ralph Fitch. Together with the rest of his party, he was interested in seeing the East, and looking at all the possibilities of doing business there. He carried with him a special letter from Elizabeth. This took the place of a passport, as it was an official letter from the Queen to Akbar, Emperor of India. The letter has been shortened and the language put into modern English. (Elizabeth can have had little knowledge of the size of Akbar's kingdom, as Cambaya was just one district forming only a small part of his empire.)

> Elizabeth by the grace of God
> To the most mighty prince, Lord Zelabdim Akbar,
> King of Cambaya.
> Our Subjects have a great desire to visit the most distant places of the world to trade with everyone wherever they can. We would consider it a courtesy done to us if you would welcome them. We have heard of your Majesty's kindness and we know you will treat them well, especially since they have made such a long and hard journey.

*Elizabeth's signature*

*Sometimes, when signing papers, she would write her name in letters as high as seven centimetres!*

Carrying this with them as proof of their identity and purpose in travelling so far away, the English merchants began their journey to the land of the Great Mughal.

# A European map of the East

*European travellers were helped by the use of new maps, such as this one, which was drawn by Mercator in the sixteenth century. When the first English ambassador to India arrived at court he presented a book to the Emperor, and this map was in it.*

**1** Find a modern map of the East and compare it with the Mercator map above. What are the main differences that you see? Why do you think these differences exist?

**2** The island of Ceylon which lies off the south eastern coast of India has another name today. What is it?

**3** Trace the outlines of the land from a modern map which shows Europe, the Middle East, Africa and Asia, and work out the overland route from the Mediterranean to the East. Pick out the easiest way of making the overland journey to India.

**4** Look up the route of the Silk Road to China, and add this to your outline map. Do some general reading on the countries the routes cross. What sort of difficulties would sixteenth-century travellers have on a caravan journey to the East?

**5** What famous towns and cities have grown up around the trade routes to the East?

**6** There are many things to discover about how people travelled across difficult stretches of land. Imagine that you are part of a caravan travelling through the Middle East to Asia, by camel train. Find out about water problems, clothes, camels, oasis stops, food and cooking utensils. You will need to look in many different books to gather all this information. This will make a very interesting research project on sixteenth-century caravan journeys.

**7** What problems did sixteenth-century sailors have to face?

**8** In what ways were they different from the problems faced by travellers going by the overland route to the East?

**9** Try making your own quill pen. The book mentioned on the next page (*Copycats*) will help you. Imagine you are either Elizabeth or Akbar, and write your own formal letter.

For further reading:
R Tames, *Exploring Other Civilisations* (Stanley Thornes, 1987)

Practical history:
M Ford, *Copycats* (André Deutsch, 1983)
In this book you will find many interesting things to make at home or at school. Here is a list of those connected with the topics within this book. Use Tudor or Mughal designs for decoration: appliqued hangings page 37; folding fans page 87; lacquer work page 78; make-up page 73; marbled papers page 7; papier-mâché page 17; pomanders page 11; quill pens page 61.

# A Muslim ruler in Hindustan

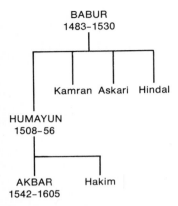

BABUR
1483–1530

Kamran  Askari  Hindal

HUMAYUN
1508–56

AKBAR      Hakim
1542–1605

*The Mughal dynasty up to Akbar*

Akbar, Emperor of India, ruled a country as large as the whole of Europe put together. Like the Tudors, the Mughal family had won the right to rule through battle. Akbar's grandfather, Babur, had invaded India from central Asia, and had overcome the resistance of the local rulers. By 1526 he had conquered a large part of northern India; but when he died Humayun, his son, proved less capable of ruling, and had to leave India for his own safety. Humayun's young son, Akbar, was left behind; and it was almost three years before they saw each other again. Humayun's brothers rose in rebellion and were hard to defeat. When Humayun finally regained his throne he was to reign for only six months, and when he died in 1556, Akbar was crowned Emperor of one of the richest countries in the sixteenth-century world.

The Mughal family were Muslims, and followed the religion of Islam. When they conquered India they realised that they were going to have to rule a country whose inhabitants were mostly Hindus. There were also Christians living in India at this time. When the Portuguese sailors found the sea route to India, the merchants who followed them settled in Goa and developed a Christian community there. Akbar was deeply interested in all ideas of religion and welcomed people who could tell him things about other ways of worship. He had to find a way of ruling that brought people together, despite differences in their ways of worship, and so he encouraged visitors to share their knowledge with him, and created an atmosphere of tolerance and understanding at his court. Akbar was unusual in the way in which he tried to overcome the religious differences in India. At this time Europe was involved in long periods of war between the Catholics and Protestants. Akbar hoped to avoid similar wars in his country.

The Portuguese in Goa had some Jesuit priests living there. They had travelled to India to try to convert the people there to Christianity. Akbar invited them to visit him at Fatehpur Sikri. Three Jesuit missionaries left Goa and reached Akbar's court in 1580. They were surprised by his friendly attitude towards them:

> Akbar receives foreigners and strangers . . . with marked courtesy and kindliness . . . especially ambassadors of foreign kings.

The people they met there thought they were quite unusual, too. One of the priests kept a diary of his life in India. His name was Anthony Monserrate. This is what he wrote about his arrival at court:

> Everyone stopped and stared in great surprise and perplexity, wondering who these strange-looking unarmed men might be, with their long black robes, their curious caps, their shaven faces and their tonsured heads.

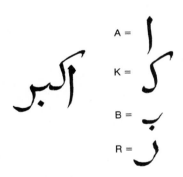

A = ا
K = ک
B = ب
R = ر

*The Arabic characters that form Akbar's name*

*Arabic is the language of the Qur'an (Koran), which is a set of scriptures giving guidelines to Muslims on how to lead their lives. The language of the Mughal court was Persian, but every Muslim had to learn Arabic in order to understand the Qur'an.*

**1** The two Jesuits in the picture were called Aquaviva and Henriques. The picture was painted in 1605, twenty-five years after Monserrate's description was written. In what way have they changed their appearance?

**2** What sort of books do you think are on the floor?

**3** The picture shows a religious discussion between Christians, Muslims and Hindus. What religious books would be available in the room?

**4** Find Akbar in the picture. Do you think he is wearing particularly kingly clothes?

**5** On what is he sitting?

**6** From reference books, find out about the Society of Jesus. Why would Jesuits be living in India at this time?

**7** Find out as much as possible about the Portuguese settlement of Goa, western India. Why was there a European settlement in India?

**8** Look at the picture below of Akbar and read the written description. Compare both pieces of evidence. Which piece of evidence tells you most about Akbar?

**9** Look at the other pictures of Akbar which you will find in the colour section at the centre of this book. In what ways is the sketch below different in style from the other pictures?

*A Mughal miniature of 1605, showing one of Akbar's discussion meetings*

The picture above of the Jesuits talking to Akbar shows the inside of a special room built behind the Mosque at Fatehpur Sikri. The Muslim holy day began at sundown on Thursday evening, and after praying and keeping Friday for special duties and lessons in the Mosque, Akbar would ask the leaders of all the religious groups who where staying at Fatehpur to join him for discussion on Friday evening. This could go on all night, as Akbar found it difficult to sleep and had an amazing amount of energy. It must have been a very demanding experience to take part in Akbar's discussion groups and keep awake!

A description of Akbar from Monserrate's diary:

> One could easily recognise . . . that he is the King. He has broad shoulders, somewhat bandy legs well suited for horsemanship, and a light brown complexion. He carries his head bent towards the right shoulder. His forehead is broad . . . his eyes so bright and flashing that they seem like a sea shimmering in the sunlight. His nose is straight and small. Between the left nostril and the upper lip there is a mole. He shaves his beard, but wears a moustache . . . He does not cut his hair, nor does he wear a hat, but a turban into which he gathers up his hair.

*A Mughal sketch of Akbar*

# Akbar's religious problem

Because he was prepared to be so tolerant, Akbar offended the strict Muslims who were at his court. They thought that he was putting aside his own religion and being too friendly towards Hindus and Christians. Monserrate wrote that Akbar would not wear Muslim dress, which he described as a long white robe of wool or cotton with low shoes:

> (Akbar) wears garments of silk, beautifully embroidered in gold . . . his boots cover his ankles completely. Moreover, he himself designed the fashion and shape of these boots. He wears gold ornaments, pearls and jewellery. He is very fond of carrying a European sword and dagger.

In an effort to make Hindus happier with Muslim rule, Akbar encouraged all those who were capable of doing well in jobs at court to come to him for employment. This ability to do a good job was the only qualification needed. Akbar did not discriminate against anyone who practised a different faith, or who came from another country. The Jesuits who came to his court were given rooms and became teachers to his sons. Hindus became trusted advisers and ran large sections of central and local government. As long as Akbar felt he could trust those around him, all were welcome to work within his Empire, and were paid good salaries.

All these things worried Akbar's Muslim advisers, who helped him make laws by looking at the Qur'an. Akbar began to reject strict Islamic ideas, and at one point even introduced a new form of religion with himself as the person to worship. Few people seemed to take this seriously, and neither did Akbar. Nonetheless, it upset many Muslims. Akbar's upbringing had not encouraged him to be a strict Muslim ruler; but while he tried to create a country where all people could feel they were free to believe in their own religion, he met opposition from others who did not share his ideas.

Religion played a large part in some other areas of Akbar's life. Like all monarchs, Akbar needed a son to inherit the Mughal Empire after his death. By the age of 26 he still had no son. All of his children had died. He asked holy men who lived as hermits to pray for him. One of these men, Shaikh Salim Christi, told him that he would have three sons; and shortly afterwards his Hindu wife, the daughter of the Raja of Amber in northwest India, became pregnant. He sent her to live with Shaikh Salim, and she gave birth to her son in the town of Sikri. (Two other sons were born later, and so the holy man's words came true.)

To honour Shaikh Salim and to celebrate the birth of his three sons, Akbar decided to build a new palace overlooking the village of Sikri. This was to be known as Fatehpur Sikri. The building of the city also coincided with the end of a successful military campaign, and became known as Akbar's 'city of victory'.

# Akbar's special city

Akbar loved being involved in practical things. He enjoyed painting and hunting, gardening and building. In the colour section at the centre of the book you can see him involved in the building of his new palace of Fatehpur Sikri. Look carefully at the picture and see if you can work out the answers to the following questions.

**1** What do you think the Indian craftsman is saying to Akbar?

**2** Can you see any rich noblemen in this picture?

**3** What are Akbar's servants carrying?

**4** To whom does the falcon belong?

**5** For what entertainment would falcons be used at court?

**6** Fatehpur Sikri was made of red sandstone. What other materials can you see being used?

**7** Look carefully at the section which shows bricks being made. Would you see pictures of English women working at a job like this in Elizabethan England?

**8** What sort of tools can you see in the picture?

**9** What animals are being used for transportation and what are they carrying?

**10** How is the scaffolding held up?

**11** There are four people carrying long sticks. For what reason would these be used?

All the workmen would be Hindus. Here is what Akbar's grandfather Babur said about Indian workmen:

> A good thing in Hindustan is that it has unnumbered and endless workmen of every kind.

**12** In the picture you can see inside some of the finished palace rooms as well as the building work being done elsewhere. What sort of jobs would have to be done by Indian workmen to make the rooms beautiful?

**13** All the work is being done by hand. How many people do you think Akbar would have to employ on the building of a palace as large as this?

**14** Note Monserrate's comment:

> Akbar is never without arms and is always surrounded, even within his private apartment, by a body guard of about twenty men, variously armed.

Can you see Akbar's bodyguard in this picture?

**15** Akbar liked to walk the streets of his towns in disguise. In this way he could gain much information about what people thought of him as a ruler. Do you think it would be dangerous for a king to travel alone?

All the following extracts come from writers of this period. (Ralph Fitch and Peter Mundy were travellers from England.) See how much you can learn about Akbar and his city of Fatehpur Sikri:

Akbar is so devoted to building that he sometimes quarries stone himself. Nor does he shrink from practising the craft of an ordinary worker. For this purpose he has built a workshop near the palace for painting, goldsmith work, tapestry making, carpet and curtain making, and the manufacture of arms. Hither he very frequently comes and relaxes his mind.

*Monserrate*

At one time he would be deeply immersed in state affairs, or giving audience to his subjects, and the next moment he would be seen shearing camels, hewing stones, cutting wood or hammering iron.

*Abul Fazl*

The splendour of his palaces approaches closely that of the royal palaces of Europe. They are magnificently built of hewn stone and are decorated both with painting and carving.

*Monserrate*

reservoirs

The King's house stands on the highest hill, within which are abundance of courts, galleries, arches, pillars, *tanks*, private rooms, all very rich, curious, and full of invention of painting, carving etc. Also a little garden.

*Mundy*

food-market

Agra and Fatehpur are two very great cities, either of them much greater than London, and very populous. Between Agra and Fatehpur are 12 miles and all the way is a *market of victuals* and other things.

*Fitch*

The city of Fatehpur Sikri today is often described as a ghost city. In fact, the palace was deserted by Akbar and his court after only fourteen years because of difficulties with water supplies. The climate of India and the red sandstone in which it was built have preserved much of Akbar's palace, so that if you visit it today you can see many things that give you information about Akbar's India.

The palace of Fatehpur Sikri is frozen in time, and is only used by pilgrims visiting the tomb of Shaik Salim Christi, by tourists who are looking at Mughal India, and by one other group of people on a special occasion every year. That group is the Muslims. All people who are Muslims are expected to obey certain rules. For Muslims there is only one God, Allah, and his truth was revealed to the prophet Muhammed in the words of the Qur'an. A devout Muslim would be expected to pray five times a day facing the holy city of Makkah (Mecca) and to make a pilgrimage there at least once in his or her lifetime. Every year, during the thirty days of Ramadan, Muslims are expected to fast and not touch either food or water during daylight hours. At the end of Ramadan comes the celebration of Eid Al-Fitr, and there is feasting, with parties and all kinds of entertainment. Every year Fatehpur Sikri comes alive with these celebrations, and Muslims go to the palace courtyard to enjoy the end of the fasting period.

**1** Find out more about the special festivals connected with the religions of Hinduism and Islam. Look in a calendar and find out when they are celebrated. Make a note of them on your classroom calendar if they are not already there. Find out how these festivals are celebrated in Britain today.

**2** Akbar's reign was recorded by two Indian historians in particular. Abul Fazl was a close friend of Akbar, and wrote two official histories which had Akbar's approval. Here is what Abul Fazl wrote about religion:

> We ought . . . to bring them all into one religion (. . . so that we would not lose) what is good in any one religion. . . . In that way honour would be rendered to God, peace would be given to the peoples, and security to the Empire.

Badaoni was a strict Muslim and because he did not approve of Akbar as King, he wrote his history in secret. So both histories are biased. Over what religious ideas would Fazl and Badaoni disagree?

**3** When you read several conflicting accounts of one event, how do you make up your mind which to believe?

---

For further reading:
P Bahree, *The Hindu World* (Macdonald, 1982)
R Tames, *A Dictionary of Islam* (Batsford, 1985)
A Kamm, *The Story of Islam* (Dinosaur Publications, 1976)
R Kelly, *A World of Change* (Stanley Thornes, 1987)

Visits:
The Victoria and Albert Museum, London (Gallery 42)
The Regents Park Mosque and Leighton House, London

---

# To entertain a king

Akbar's grandfather, Babur, wrote in his diary:

> In that charmless and disorderly *Hind* [India], plots of garden were laid out with order and symmetry . . . and in every border rose and narcissus in perfect arrangement.

All the Mughal Emperors loved gardens. Babur found the climate of India very hot and the land very barren. He decided to give himself cool, refreshing surroudings. Akbar enjoyed building palaces and forts more than designing gardens, but he used the garden spaces created by his grandfather for entertainment and relaxation.

Islam as a religion grew out of the hot desert area of the Middle East. In the Qur'an heaven is a garden of beautiful flowers, trees and cool running water. Islamic Kings tried to create this idea on earth too, and the design of their gardens followed a basic shape. We can see some of the things that Mughal Emperors liked by looking at the pictures drawn by court artists.

*A jar and cover from 1700*

*An eighteenth-century box*

*A Mughal prayer rug:
seventeenth-century*

Some Mughal miniatures have been included in the colour section at the centre of this book.

Islamic gardens were laid out in careful geometric shapes. Muslims believe that only Allah and not humans can create life, so artists, craftsmen and designers worked with all kinds of patterns to represent life and its various forms. You can see that this idea has gone into many different things. On this page and on page 37 are drawings of several objects which can be seen in the Victoria and Albert Museum in London. Objects like these could often be found in Mughal palaces or in rich Muslim households.

How many different patterns can you see? (Look carefully at all the borders, rims, flowers, leaves and curves. You will be surprised by the number of repeating shapes you can find.)

**1** Why do we preserve things in museums?

**2** Who decides what a museum will buy to add to its collection?

**3** How many objects from England and India which date back to the time of Elizabeth and Akbar have you seen in museums?

**4** Many of the objects you will see in this book would have belonged to wealthy people. Why do we have so few examples of things which belonged to poor people?

**5** Keeping things safe for hundreds of years is difficult. Which of the objects shown in the pictures would be damaged most easily? What methods are used to preserve them?

**6** Why do so few textiles survive for us to look at?

**7** In the Victoria and Albert Museum there is a coat which belonged to a Mughal emperor. It has embroidery all over it. What sort of animals, birds and flowers do you think would be sewn on the coat of an Indian emperor?

**8** The peacock is the national bird of India and roams wild there. In what ways would both Elizabeth and Akbar use the peacock for their costumes either as a design, or in colours, or in feathers?

*A piece of a shawl from the late seventeenth century/early eighteenth century*

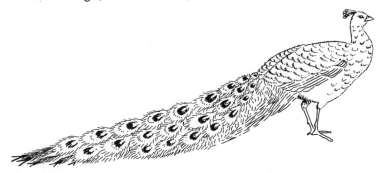

**9** There are many pictures of both Elizabeth and Akbar within this book. Design costumes for them for an evening's entertainment at a feast. Use collage materials for a large wall display.

## The gardens of Mughal India

We have looked at the kind of designs which decorated the many things you could see in the house or palace of a wealthy person. Now imagine an Islamic garden designed in the same way, with water channels running in straight lines to the middle, and walls enclosing the courtyard for privacy. Reservoirs were designed to provide water for the plants, and fountains kept the air fresh in the heat of an Indian summer. Gardens were designed to be open-air rooms on a huge scale. Many pictures show Indian kings seated in a garden on a beautiful carpet, under a canopy, enjoying the company of family or friends. On many occasions a garden would be used to entertain visitors from other countries, and large feasts were held. Jugglers, dancers and musicians would be invited in to amuse everyone there. Shaded from the heat by embroidered canopies of silk, and surrounded by cool trees and flowers, Akbar could see to the affairs of state, dictate to secretaries and welcome friends. The gardens of the Mughal emperors were also designed for the pleasure of the women of the court, and part of the area would be specially secluded to allow them freedom to enjoy themselves. At night-time the gardens must have looked especially beautiful; torches would be lit, glimmering through the fall of the water from the fountains. Travellers from England would have been delighted to see gardens very like their own, and similarly laid out in formal patterns with tree walks and fountains. (In an Elizabethan garden water was often used to play practical jokes on passers-by! This did not happen in an Islamic garden.)

The seventeenth-century traveller in India, Peter Mundy, wrote in his diary:

> The Gardens about Agra are many ... in some, little groves of trees, as Apple trees ... Orange trees, Mulberry trees, Mango trees, Cocoa trees, Fig trees, *Plantain* trees ... In other squares are your flowers, herbs, whereof Roses, Marigolds ... Poppie red, *carnation* and white; and divers other sorts of fair flowers which we know not in our parts.

*Plantain* a type of banana
*carnation* pink

Akbar's favourite 'garden', however, was a great deal larger than any Mughal palace garden. Akbar conquered more territory after he became Emperor. The people of Kashmir ignored his power, and Akbar invaded their country in 1586. He won a rich and fertile area which had a refreshing climate. He enjoyed the autumn season most, and travelled back to Kashmir three times in his life. He called it his private garden, and enjoyed travelling by boat among floating gardens. As his boat drifted downstream, it was followed by a thousand more which carried his family, friends and every member of the court. From Akbar's 'garden' of Kashmir came a lot of money, from the sale of saffron; and from other Mughal gardens sandalwood and rose oils were produced. Fruit trees provided the Emperor's table with a wide choice of fruit at all times of the year, and herbs were grown to give taste to other main dishes.

# Making your own Islamic patterns

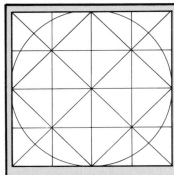

### A geometric design

You will need paper, a pencil, ruler and a compass. Draw a square and divide it up in any way you wish. Make sure you are accurate in what you draw. Try using blue, yellow and green for colouring in this basic pattern.

### A rotating design

Work on your pattern in rough first. The example given shows leaves of various shapes. Try experimenting with your own design and imagine how it will look when you have traced it four times into one whole pattern.

Next you will need cartridge paper and tracing paper. Divide a square of cartridge paper into four equal parts. Fit your tracing paper over the top right hand square and draw on your design. Hold your tracing paper firmly or use paper clips. Trace and turn your paper. If you are careful and accurate in what you do you will find you have a perfectly matched outline to colour.

In group work make a set of paper tile patterns for display on your classroom wall. Design the whole picture first and then work on individual squares. Use a garden theme with plants, animals and birds.

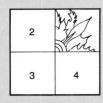

Here is a list of flowers that you might see in a Mughal garden:

poppies; roses; marigolds; hyacinths; violets; zinnias; wallflowers; hollyhocks; delphiniums.

Some of these flowers you will know, others you may need to look up. Complete your tile display by adding a border.

◼ Imagine you are in the group of people that set sail from England in 1583. Travelling with Ralph Fitch from Goa to Fatehpur Sikri you arrive at Akbar's court and are sent an invitation to join an evening feast in the gardens there. Write a diary account of the evening's entertainment commenting in particular on the following:

the evening meal, clothes, entertainers, the garden surroundings, Akbar and his court circle.

Akbar enjoyed all open-air activities. As a young boy he often played truant from lessons to take part in sports. He rode fierce camels, and throughout his life enjoyed being on fighting elephants. He risked his life many times, but ignored the dangers and continued to take part in competitive adventures.

# Hunting in Mughal India

When a hunt was organised, it was a major event. The whole court of the Muhgal Emperor went with Akbar on an expedition, including his wives. The women of the royal household were carefully guarded, so they travelled in special litters called *palanquins* which had curtains surrounding them. This was to make sure that they were not seen by anyone. Often the curtains were made of gold mesh, through which the travellers could see but not be seen. Sometimes they travelled in a *howdah* on top of an elephant. Coaches, horsemen, and elephants of state all moved along in the procession, with the Emperor's banner prominently flying at the head of it.

*A woman in a palanquin*

On the left of the picture below you can see a Muslim woman on a horse. She is wearing a garment which covers the whole of her body. It is called being in *purdah*. In some Muslim countries women still dress in this way. On the right you can see a Hindu woman on an ox. She is dressed in a sari, which is the traditional dress for most women in India. At the top of the picture you can see a camel and elephants transporting the Emperor's household belongings. These pictures were drawn by Peter Mundy, who saw Akbar's grandson make a royal progress in 1632. They show the Emperor in a litter as well as some other parts of the progress. The design of the Mughal seal, which was on the banners, has been enlarged and copied on the next page so that you can see it clearly.

*How women travelled in Mughal India*

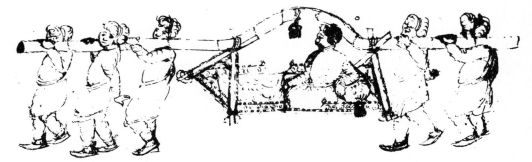

*Mundy's eye-witness drawing of the Mughal Emperor in 1632*

The Emperor often planned his travels with more than just a sporting holiday in mind. When Akbar heard that there might be a rebellion in his kingdom, he moved his court to that area and set up camp. The army moved with him, and as soon it was known that Akbar had arrived with his soldiers any attempt at rebellion was soon forgotten. An official hunt also kept his army fit and in regular training. If there was no war in which to fight, his soldiers would get bored and restless. One way of making certain they were well-disciplined was to keep them busy, and so official hunts were organised.

This is what Abul Fazl wrote about the army:

> A monarch should ever be intent on conquest, otherwise his neighbours rise in arms against him. The army should be exercised in warfare, lest for want of training they become self-indulgent.

Akbar's soldiers would ride ahead of the main court. When they arrived at their destination the Emperor's great pavillion would be set up, and the many hundreds of other tents would form a protective ring around him. To prepare for the hunt, the army would enclose an area sometimes as large as sixty miles wide, and would drive the animals inwards until they were trapped in a small space. Akbar and his close friends would then move in for the kill. Thousands of animals would be slaughtered and everyone, in order of rank, would be allowed to take part. On one occasion the slaughter was so great that Akbar turned away and refused to kill any more animals. After this he rarely hunted in such a way again. This must have seemed strange to his friends, as hunting was a traditional pastime for wealthy people.

*The Mughal seal*

Akbar's favourite form of hunting was with his cheetahs. He was fascinated by them. They travelled to the hunt on litters, dressed in jewelled coats, and blindfolded. Like his hawks, the cheetahs were trained to hunt, kill and return with the prey. Other favourite hunting animals included dogs, and English hunting dogs were given as presents to the Mughal emperors. It was difficult to know what to give to one of the wealthiest men in the world. The diaries of English travellers who were on business in India tell of the worries they had about this: would their presents be considered impressive or amusing enough to be accepted? If they were not good enough, they might not be allowed to see the Emperor.

Turn to the colour pictures in the centre-section and find the one of Akbar hunting in an enclosure. Compare it with the picture of Akbar in the previous chapter. See if you can recognise the Emperor in the hunting scene.

**1** With what weapons is he armed?

**2** What impression do you get of this picture?

**3** A miniature painting of this sort of subject cannot be an 'eye-witness report', as a painter could not draw this as quickly as a camera could take a picture nowadays. Do you think it is reliable evidence?

**4** How is the hunting organised?

**5** Who has been allowed into the enclosure?

**6** Hunting was a favourite sport of all sixteenth-century monarchs. Do you think that hunting is approved of in the same way in the twentieth century?

Elizabeth hunted animals differently. Her huntsmen trapped the best animals in an area and presented them to her. She picked the ones she wanted, and then they were set free for the chase. Elizabeth enjoyed hunting, although it was considered a male sport, and she was an extremely good horsewoman. Look at pictures of Elizabeth in other books. You will find plenty of illustrations of her enjoying picnics which were often held after hunting.

**7** Compare the different styles of hunting dress of Elizabeth and Akbar. Look at the huge skirt Elizabeth had to wear. This was called a farthingale.

**8** Do you think Elizabeth would have found it difficult to hunt in a farthingale?

**9** Write your own story about a hunting scene, and add illustrations to it. You will need to think about a camp site, styles of hunting, different animals, accidents and injuries, the landscape and forests and the atmosphere of the chase. It should be an exciting story but you will need to prepare your work carefully. You could end your story with a description of an open-air feast around a camp fire.

---

For further reading from the India Book House (see page 50):
*The Great Mughals,* Books 1 and 2
*Tales of Birbal*

Things to do:
BBC computer program, *Design your own Islamic pattern*

Visit:
The Victoria and Albert Museum (Gallery 41)

---

# The world of the Great Mughal

Although Europe and India were thousands of miles apart, those in power behaved in similar ways. Both Elizabeth and Akbar kept control of their countries through the force of their powerful personalities. At times there were rebellions, and some assassination attempts. Both of them survived by being careful to keep the affection of most of the people that they ruled, and by taking sensible safety precautions. Large scale hunts and progresses were part of an important public relations act, and daily life at court followed this pattern also.

## Daily life and state business

Akbar's day began at sunrise when court musicians began to play. He would then pray and prepare for the first public duty of the day. This was to show himself to his people on the Balcony of Appearances. People would crowd round to catch a glimpse of the King and offer him petitions. After this Akbar went back to bed for a few hours, before inspecting the troops and army animals. At twelve o'clock elephant fights, acrobatics or jugglers would entertain the Emperor until he had more formal duties to which to attend. Monserrate described the elephant fights:

> The Indians train elephants to fight. There are indeed extraordinary numbers of elephants in the royal camps and cities ... most of the males are trained for battle and are furnished with defensive armour, though indeed they are quite as dangerous without this ...

> If two or more (elephants) have conceived a mutual dislike, they attack each other on sight ... they never look up towards, much less hurt, the keepers who ride upon them ... when the King is looking on at the Circus, he is protected from the elephants by a bodyguard of soldiers ... if an elephant attacks the King these men interpose themselves.

Akbar enjoyed elephant fights and was very skilled as a rider.

After this, Akbar would retire to the Hall of Private Audience, where the essential tasks of government were carried out. Here, in the centre of the Hall, on a circular platform at the top of a pillar high above the floor, sat the Emperor. Those who were closest to him were invited to go up on to a balcony. Four walkways led from this balcony to the top of the pillar, and

*Indian acrobats drawn by Mundy*

those who were summoned to speak with Akbar would make their way along these walkways to the pillar.

Those who were not included in the discussion would remain below, where they could hear what was said, even if they were not allowed to join in. The discussion would revolve around affairs of state, and the King would have his advisers ready if he needed expert help, although he did not have to accept the advice they gave. Machiavelli, who was an Italian writer, wrote about kingship. This is what he said about making decisions:

> A Prince should always seek advice. But he should do so when he wants to, not when others want him to.

In many ways Akbar fits his idea of a European Renaissance ruler.

Akbar's secretaries took down every word of the discussion, and recorded the decisions made. To run an empire as enormous as Akbar's required a large staff. The Emperor employed about six thousand officials, whose responsibilities ranged from collecting taxes and running local government to supervising the cooking in the state palaces and the organisation of Akbar's library.

Running this sort of administration required people who were well educated. All the Mughal kings valued education; but of them all, Akbar was the only one who could neither read nor write. This was partly because he had had a very unsettled childhood, and also because he disliked his lessons. He escaped whenever he could to hunt or ride or fly his pigeons. This is what Monserrate wrote of the King's amusements:

> Akbar is greatly devoted to hunting though not equally so to hawking. As he is of a somewhat morose disposition he amuses himself with various games ... They are the following:- Polo, elephant fighting, buffalo fighting, stag fighting and cock fighting, boxing contests, battles of gladiators and the flying of *tumbler pigeons* [pigeons that turn backward somersaults in the air].

> *Not a little* [much] is added to the beauty of the palaces by charming pigeoncotes. ... The pigeons are controlled at will, when they are flying, by means of certain signals ... It will seem little short of miraculous when I affirm that when sent out, they dance, turn somersaults all together in the air, fly in orderly rhythm, and return to their starting point, all at the sound of a whistle.

It seems that Akbar continued to enjoy all the things he escaped to do in his childhood, although he probably had less time to take part in sports. The fact that he had an excellent memory and listened carefully to what people had told him made up to a great extent for his lack of education. His ability to understand and remember facts helped him to make decisions without too much difficulty. In the evening he had books read to

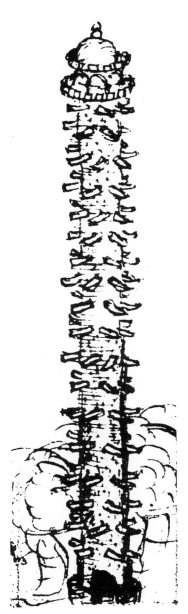

*A tower said to have been erected on the grave of one of Akbar's favourite elephants*

*Pieces of white marble in the shape of elephants' teeth projected from it. From the top of this tower the court women watched the elephant fights.*

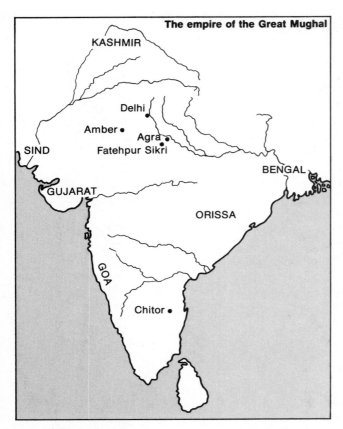

The empire of the Great Mughal

KASHMIR

SIND

GUJARAT

Delhi

Amber

Agra

Fatehpur Sikri

BENGAL

ORISSA

GOA

Chitor

*When Akbar died in 1605, all the places marked on the map above were controlled by his army and ruled by him (see page 48).*

him to broaden his knowledge, and always marked the page where the reader stopped himself; he was able to talk on many subjects so that it would not have been obvious from his conversation that he had never received a full education and could neither read nor write. He took great pleasure in the organisation of an enormous library, which contained books from many other countries. They were translated so that he could have them read to him.

Akbar impressed all those who met him with his ability as King; and even those who disliked his methods and criticised his beliefs, found it difficult to justify their attitude. Abul Fazl commented on Akbar's library:

> His Majesty's library is divided into several parts ... Prose books, poetical works, Hindi, Persian, Greek, Kashmirian, Arabic, are all separately placed ... Experienced people bring them daily and read them before his Majesty.

In the evening after the end of the formal discussion in the Hall of Private Audience, the lamps would be lit and Akbar would dine alone. On special occasions there would be a public feast, but mostly he preferred to eat in private. As many as forty different dishes would be served, each separately wrapped and sealed to prevent his food being poisoned. Akbar ate little, drank water rather then wine, and slept badly. As we have seen, the evening entertainment that gave him most pleasure was discussion and reading, which would go on into the early hours of the morning.

The Emperor's wives were a powerful influence at court. Under Qur'anic law a Muslim is allowed four wives, providing each woman is treated equally and all of the children are well provided for. Akbar had many beautiful women given to him as presents; the *zenana*, or women's apartments, contained about three hundred women who could be considered unofficial wives, and perhaps as many as five thousand women altogether. Of these women, some were members of the family, others controlled the administration of the zenana, or were servants, or guards. Those who were particular favourites were very powerful women at court. Although they were hidden behind screens, visitors were aware of the presence of the women who talked about them to each other in many different languages. They were enormously wealthy in their own right, as each had an allowance from the Emperor and could spend it as they wished. Muslim women controlled all the property that belonged to them before their marriage, and sometimes they ran businesses of their own and grew even wealthier. Although they were carefully guarded and were not allowed to take an open part in court life, they were influential in politics and could not be ignored. English ambassadors like Sir Thomas Roe soon discovered that if they won favour with the King's favourite wives, they would get an audience with the King.

There were special occasions for which huge feasts were designed. There were the New Year celebrations, and the Emperor's birthday on which he would be weighed against gold, silver, jewels, cloths and food. Sir Thomas Roe, England's first ambassador to India, saw this ceremony taking place, and wrote about it in his diary. Compare Roe's description to the Mughal miniature which you will find in the colour section at the centre of this book:

> Here attended the Nobility, all sitting about [the scales] on Carpets, until the King came; who at last appeared clothed, or rather laden with diamonds, Rubies, Pearls, and other precious vanities, so great, so glorious! . . . Suddenly he entered into the scales, sat like a woman on her legs, and there were put in against him many bags to fit his weight, which were changed six times, and they say was silver, . . . almost one thousand pound sterling. After with Gold and Jewels and with precious stones . . . Then against Cloth of Gold, Silk, Stuffs, Linen.

Another special court ceremony was held in the spring. This was the occasion on which Akbar presented new honours and promotions, and the celebrations could last for up to twenty days. Each day the Emperor was invited to a house or a tent, and would give and receive presents. Feasting, singing and dancing took place, and on the final day the wives of the nobility would join the Emperor's zenana so that all the women could celebrate together.

# The power of a Mughal monarch

Machiavelli wrote this about kingly power:

> Nothing brings a prince more prestige than great campaigns and striking demonstrations of his personal abilities.

Akbar was a very tolerant ruler, but in an age which gave kings great power he could also be very harsh. In order to prove his kingship to everyone, he had to be constantly aware of the possibility of rebellion and see the way to crush it. At 19 he lost his temper with his foster brother who had betrayed him. (It is possible that Akbar had learned of an assassination plot.) He

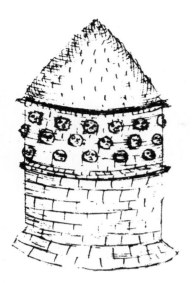

A sixteenth-century monarch deals with rebellion. This picture is from Peter Mundy's diary.

knocked his brother unconscious, and then had him thrown to his death from a balcony. When the Hindu Rajputs rose in rebellion at Chitor, he laid seige to their fortress until they surrendered. Look at the picture of the tower of heads. This shows the fate of the Hindu Rajputs.

Such behaviour was not typical; Akbar normally attempted peaceful relationships through marriages or treaties. However, if this was not possible, he used his armies. In 1573 he took Gujarat; in 1576, Bengal; and in 1586 Kashmir was added to his Empire. By 1592 he had turned to Orissa, and in 1595 Sind fell to him. By 1600 the Mughal Empire was as large as Europe, and was still expanding when Akbar died in 1605.

**1** The date is 1586 and you are visiting Fatehpur Sikri to present a petition to Akbar. You join the crowds flocking in to watch the circus entertainment. Akbar arrives on a white elephant in a great procession. The afternoon's performances include elephant fighting, gladiator sports, boxing and polo. Describe the scene around you, or draw a series of pictures showing the afternoon's events.

**2** The people that Elizabeth and Akbar ruled had to be reminded just how powerful their rulers were. Here are some examples of how they sought to promote their public image:

Hunting, feasting, progresses, coins and seals, birthday celebrations, clothes, palaces, pictures, gardens.

Pick two of these examples and explain how Elizabeth and Akbar made use of them to show themselves as they wished to be seen.

**3** Both Elizabeth and Akbar had to make difficult decisions as part of their job as ruler. Here are some examples from Elizabeth's reign:

*A family problem* — Mary Queen of Scots
*A personal problem* — the rebellion of the Earl of Essex
*A national problem* — the rebellion of the Northern Lords
*An empire problem* — the war in Ireland
*An international problem* — the Spanish Armada.

Find out as much as possible about all of these, and then use the chapters in this book to find out about some of the problems Akbar had to deal with. How did he solve them?

**4** Despite the differences in the societies they ruled, there were some things that Elizabeth and Akbar had in common with each other. If you had to pick one thing from the examples given in this book, what would it be?

For further reading:
J Harrison, *Akbar and the Mughal Empire* (Greenhaven Press, 1980)
*Colouring Mughal Miniatures* (Bodleian Library Publication, 1981)

# The growth of big business

The growth and stability of Akbar's India encouraged trade and industry. Akbar welcomed new trade links with the Europeans. He wanted to provide an outlet for the export of goods produced in India; an increased demand for these would provide more employment for his people. The cotton industry in Gujarat and Bengal was well established, and the colour-fast fabrics produced there could find a market outside the area of the Indian Ocean. Monsoons and periodic droughts caused widespread famines, and if money could be made through European trade, this might provide help in times of hardship.

The 'big business' of the sixteenth century lay, at first, in the four fine spices of cloves, nutmeg, mace and cinnamon, as well as in pepper. European merchants then found that they could extend their trade to buying and selling to all the empires of the East. Portuguese, Dutch and English ships went to China and Japan, and bought silk, tea, opium, chinaware and silver. These goods were exchanged in India and the Middle East for other luxury goods such as carpets, cotton pieces, perfumes and jewels. The famous East India Company was founded in England in 1600, and over the following years it was to introduce new ideas to members of the English upper classes. After the East India ships had finished trading in the East, they came home to England with cargoes of luxury goods. By the middle of the eighteenth century it was possible to buy all kinds of items from the East India Company shops, and so it became fashionable to use spices when cooking, to wear clothes made of silk and cotton, and to drink tea and coffee out of china cups. The East India Company became one of the richest trading companies in England. The high prices that they charged for their goods meant that the poorer classes could not afford to buy them at this time. This pattern of trade, and the change in fashionable habits which came as a result of European merchants trading in the East, was only one of the many cultural influences which the East had on the people of the West. There was a whole new world of science and medicine, philosophy and scholarship, art, music and industry to discover. Many of these influences form part of the way of life that we take for granted in Britain today.

# Find out more for yourself

There are many ways of finding out more about the age of Elizabeth. Your local library and school library will provide you with a wide range of books from which to choose; and if you use the bibliographies carefully they will help you select information on areas of specialist interest. The pictures included will lead you to places such as Hatfield House and the Victoria and Albert Museum, both of which have many paintings and other objects associated with Elizabeth. The National Portrait Gallery contains Tudor portraits amongst its collection of pictures of important British people.

Finding out about Mughal India is less easy. There are fewer books available on Indian history than on Elizabethan history. Both the British Museum and the Victoria and Albert Museum have Indian galleries, and you can contact the Education Departments of both. The India Office Library and Records at Blackfriars, London; the External Services Division at the School of Oriental and African Studies, London University; and the Commonwealth Institute will be very helpful for pictures, project advice and extra reading. Books from the Indian Book House can be obtained from Books from India, 45 Museum Street, London.

Perhaps you would like to include a visit to a mosque or a Hindu temple as part of your studies. (But please write or phone in advance to see if it is convenient!) The Islamic Cultural Foundation will be able to give you advice on this, and on extra reading material. You may find it more difficult to find out more about Akbar himself, but the places listed above will give you some help, and you can look yourself for facts about the whole world of Islam, as well as India itself.

# Index

# Acknowledgements

The author and publishers wish to thank the following for permission to reproduce material:

Ashmolean Museum, page 21; BBC Hulton Picture Library, pages 30, 41, 42, 44, 45 and 48; British Museum, pages 3, 18, and 28; Chester Beatty Library, page 28; Christina Gascoigne, page 33; College of Arms, page 12; Countess Beauchamp, page 26; Marquess of Bath, Longleat House, Warminster, Wiltshire, page 26; Marquess of Salisbury and the Courtauld Institute of Art, page 19; National Portrait Gallery, page 25; Victoria & Albert Museum, front cover and pages 18, 19, 26, 27 and 28. The miniature of Elizabeth I on page 4 is reproduced with the gracious permission of Her Majesty the Queen. The Arabic characters on page 32 were reproduced by Mr Aziz Ahmed.

Every effort has been made to contact copyright holders, but we apologise if any have been overlooked.

# A World of Change

This book is part of a series entitled *A World of Change*, intended for the 11–14 age group. The aim of the whole series is to combine a firm framework of historical fact with a 'skill-based' approach. The factual content provides continuity, and the opportunity to study causation and development. It is balanced by the two other vital ingredients for lively study of history: opportunity for 'empathy', which enables children to make an imaginative leap into the past; and study of a variety of original sources, both written and visual.

The series comprises a core textbook which studies a number of themes important in the Early Modern Age, approximately 1450–1700; a number of linked topic books; and a teacher's book for the whole series (which includes copyright-free worksheets).

The core book is primarily concerned with the British Isles, but within the context of what was happening in the rest of the world, known and unknown. The well-known political, religious and economic themes are considered. So too are the lives of ordinary men, women and children, and the way in which both change and continuity affected them. The book does not set out to be a full chronological survey, but it is hoped that it is sufficiently flexible to be used in that way if desired.

The core textbook is complete in itself, but has also been designed to provide a number of stepping-off points for 'patch studies'. Opportunities for this kind of work are provided by the eight *World of Change* topic books which are clearly linked to the themes in the main book. However, the topic books are also designed so that they can be used on their own if desired. All the topic books are listed on the back cover.

# For the teacher

The use of primary sources can present some problems at this level. It is hoped that there is a reasonable balance between written and visual evidence, and that the text provides the student with enough concrete information for further clarification. Both written and visual sources have been carefully selected, and only occasionally paraphrased.

Further notes on the use of this book can be found in the Teacher's Book for the whole *World of Change* series.

Some suggestions for useful background reading:
C Erickson, *The First Elizabeth* (Macmillan, 1983)
P Williams, *The Tudor Regime* (Clarendon Press, Oxford, 1979)
R Strong, *The Cult of Elizabeth* (Thames and Hudson, 1977)
C Camden, *The Elizabethan Woman: a panorama of English womanhood, 1540–1640* (Cleaver Hume Press, 1952)
R A Houlbrooke, *The English Family 1450–1700* (Longman, 1984)
L Binyon, *Akbar* (Thomas Nelson, 1939)
G Hambley, *The Cities of Mughal India* (Elek Books, 1968)
B Gascoigne, *The Great Mughuls* (Jonathan Cape, 1971)
P Pal, *Court Painting of India 16th–19th centuries* (Navin Kumar, 1983)
R Godden, *Gulbaden* (Macmillan, 1980)
N Patnaik, *A Second Paradise: Indian Courtly Life, 1590–1947* (Sidgwick and Jackson, 1985)

First published in 1987 by:
Stanley Thornes (Publishers) Ltd
Old Station Drive
Leckhampton
CHELTENHAM GL53 0DN
England

Typeset by Tech-Set, Gateshead, Tyne & Wear
Printed and bound in Great Britain by
Ebenezer Baylis and Son Ltd, Worcester

British Library Cataloguing in Publication Data

Wigner, Annabel
    Elizabeth and Akbar: portraits of power.
    1. England—Court and courtiers
    2. England—Social life and customs—
    16th century    3. Great Britain—History—
    Elizabeth, 1558–1603    4. India—Court and
    courtiers    5. India—History—1506–1765
    I. Title
    942.05'5        DA356

    ISBN 0-85950-541-3